Bible
Memory Plan
for Kids

Bible
Memory Plan
for Kids

Pamela L.
McQuade

BARBOUR
PUBLISHING

ISBN 978-1-62416-147-6

Published by Barbour Publishing, Inc., P.O. Box 719, Uhrichsville, Ohio
44683 www.barbourbooks.com

*Our mission is to publish and distribute inspirational products offering
exceptional value and biblical encouragement to the masses.*

Member of the
Evangelical Christian
Publishers Association

Printed in the United States of America.
Offset Paperback Manufacturers, Dallas, PA 18612; September 2013; D10004119

Introduction

Bible Memory Plan for Kids is designed to help your family incorporate Bible memorization into your devotional time. It provides guidelines for parents as well as ideas that can be tailored to your child's abilities and your family's style.

To help kids remember the verses they're learning, you might want to do some activities with them: Have your child draw pictures of the verses, where they lend themselves to that; use a Bible dictionary (especially an illustrated one) to discover more about the time when the scriptures were written; or have your child answer the questions that accompany each chapter of this book. Using an English dictionary might also be helpful, especially if your child is younger and you need to explain the meaning of words.

The verses in *Bible Memory Plan for Kids* are arranged topically and follow a logical pattern of Christian growth:

Weeks 1–8: Knowing God
Weeks 9–23: Saved by God
Weeks 24–27: God's Word
Weeks 28–37: Strengthened by God
Weeks 39–52: Walking with God

If it helps your family, though, you might prefer to select shorter verses to start memorization, then move on to longer ones as you and your kids become comfortable with the process.

All the verses in this book are good for your child to know, but the order in which they are memorized is not critical. If you follow the topical method, your child should begin to understand certain concepts as you move through them. If you learn the verses out of their given order, it may help to memorize contiguous verses in successive weeks. To keep the larger Bible themes in your kids' minds, take time to review other verses in the same section.

Three versions of each Bible verse are provided here. You may want to memorize the version your church uses most often so that your child will connect easily with what is taught there. Or for younger children, you may want to consider the New Life Version, an easy-to-understand, limited-vocabulary Bible.

Although fifty-two verses are provided here, I have also given a few additional suggestions at the back of the book. Parents who follow the verses provided should have plenty for a year, but there is no reason to stop memorization at that time. Feel free to extend the plan by adding these verses after Week 52!

PAMELA L. MCQUADE

Week 1

Bible Memory Verse

In the beginning God created
the heaven and the earth.
Genesis 1:1 KJV

In the beginning God created
the heavens and the earth.
Genesis 1:1 NIV

In the beginning God created
the heavens and the earth.
Genesis 1:1 NLT

About This Verse

These words begin the Bible and describe the beginning of God's creation. Encourage your child to take joy in the things God has made.

Memorization Guideline

Consider the way your child learns most easily and focus on that method in at least part of your memorization time. Some people learn better by reading, others by hearing. There is no wrong way to learn. Work within your child's "wiring" to make memorization easier.

Learning Tip

Older students may memorize Genesis 1:1–3 instead of only verse 1.

Going Deeper

Help your child understand this verse by asking these questions. Suggested responses follow in parentheses.

What does this verse tell you about God? (That He existed before anything was made, that He created everything.)

Think about what it was like when there was nothing but God. How does it make you feel? Can you imagine making everything out of nothing? What do you think about God being able to do that? (Let your children feel the awesomeness of God and His creation.)

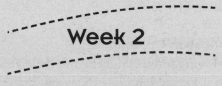

Week 2

Bible Memory Verse

In the beginning was the Word, and the Word
was with God, and the Word was God.
The same was in the beginning with God.
John 1:1–2 KJV

In the beginning was the Word, and the
Word was with God, and the Word was God.
He was with God in the beginning.
John 1:1–2 NIV

In the beginning the Word already existed.
The Word was with God, and the Word was God.
He existed in the beginning with God.
John 1:1–2 NLT

About These Verses

These are the first verses of John's Gospel. They describe a beginning even earlier than Genesis 1:1—the time when God alone existed.

Memorization Guideline

Before having your child memorize these verses, you may want to read John 1:1–18, so you can discuss the *Word* these verses talk about.

Learning Tips

Make sure you do Bible memorization in a quiet room, at a time when there will be few interruptions. Take the dog out before you start. Turn off or ignore all phones. Don't answer the doorbell until you are completely finished.

Going Deeper

Who is this mysterious Word? Children who are good readers can search out the mystery in the first part of John 1. The answer is found in verses 14–18: Jesus.

Why do you think Jesus is described as the Word? Isn't that a funny thing to call Him? (Allow the child to give opinions.)

What do you do with words? (Communicate with others.)

How does God show you what He's like? (Through sending Jesus to show Himself to you.)

Doesn't God communicate to you through Jesus? (Yes.) *Then isn't He a word?*

Older students may compare these verses and Genesis 1:1. *How are these passages the same?* (They talk about beginnings.)

How do they differ? (This is God in the beginning, not the start of creation.)

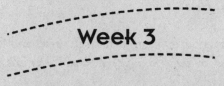

Week 3

Bible Memory Verse

And thou shalt love the Lord thy God with all thy heart, and with all thy soul, and with all thy mind, and with all thy strength: this is the first commandment.
Mark 12:30 KJV

"Love the Lord your God with all your heart and with all your soul and with all your mind and with all your strength."
Mark 12:30 NIV

"And you must love the LORD your God with all your heart, all your soul, all your mind, and all your strength."
Mark 12:30 NLT

About This Verse

This is the first of two commandments Jesus gave to a curious scribe who heard Jesus wisely disputing with the Sadducees (Jewish religious leaders) and wanted to know which commandment was most important.

Memorization Guideline

Be sure your child understands what a verse means. If you have multiple children, an older child may enjoy helping the younger ones to understand the meaning of the verse.

Learning Tips

Next week will focus on the second most important commandment. After memorizing this week's verse, you may want to read Mark 12:31 with your child, to complete the idea that Jesus was trying to get across to the scribe.

Going Deeper

Jesus says we should love God with four things. What are they? (All our heart, soul, mind, and strength.)

If you love God with those four things, will any part of you not love Him? (No.)

Then what is Jesus saying in this verse? (That we should love Him with our whole beings.)

How can you love God this way? (By putting our emotions, spirit, mind, and physical strength into loving Him. All we do should be for Him.)

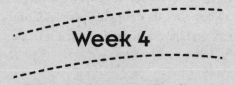

Week 4

Bible Memory Verse

And the second is like, namely this, Thou shalt love thy neighbour as thyself. There is none other commandment greater than these.
Mark 12:31 KJV

"The second is this: 'Love your neighbor as yourself.' There is no commandment greater than these."
Mark 12:31 NIV

"The second is equally important: 'Love your neighbor as yourself.' No other commandment is greater than these."
Mark 12:31 NLT

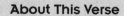

About This Verse

When the curious scribe wanted to know which commandment was most important, Jesus gave him two. The first (last week's memory verse), focused on loving God. This week's verse focuses on loving people. Combining the two, you have a picture of what it means to be a faithful Christian.

Memorization Guideline

Spend some extra time in memory work this week and review the past verses. You can review one each day, after memorizing this verse, and use the extra days to go over verses that your child seems rusty on. It's a good idea to regularly set some time aside (perhaps every couple of weeks or once a month) to review previous verses.

Learning Tips

This is a continuation of last week's verse. Review that verse. Make it clear to your children that the "second" referred to here is a second commandment.

Going Deeper

Last week's verse focused on loving God. This week talks about loving people. Why would Jesus say they were both important? (Because if you love God, you will also love the people He puts in your life.)

Can you love God and not love people? (No. We all may have trouble loving people at times, but we should be growing in our ability to love them because God loves them.)

Why would Jesus say these are the most important commandments? (Because between them, they describe what it is to be a Christian and what the Ten Commandments tell us to do to obey God.)

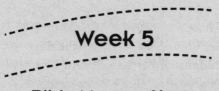

Week 5

Bible Memory Verse

For God so loved the world, that he gave his only
begotten Son, that whosoever believeth in him should
not perish, but have everlasting life.
John 3:16 KJV

"For God so loved the world that he gave his one
and only Son, that whoever believes in him shall not
perish but have eternal life."
John 3:16 NIV

"For God loved the world so much that he gave his
one and only Son, so that everyone who believes in
him will not perish but have eternal life."
John 3:16 NLT

About This Verse

This verse, perhaps the best-known in the whole Bible, speaks of the exchange between God and humanity that brings salvation to His children. God the Father sacrificed His only Son, Jesus, so each of us could have a relationship with Him. God's part is the giving. Our part is to receive the truth that we are sinners and that Jesus, the innocent One, took our punishment so that God's justice would be satisfied. Then we can live at peace with Him forever.

Memorization Guideline

Many people have memorized this verse, but have they experienced what it means? Make sure your child knows that God is calling each of us to a personal relationship with and commitment to Him.

Learning Tips

Don't let your child become overwhelmed by a longer verse. Memorize verses piece by piece, dividing them into phrases and memorizing parts of the verse day by day. Be sure to review the past memorization so that your child will not forget or disassociate one part of the verse from another.

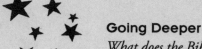

Going Deeper

What does the Bible mean when it says that Jesus is God's one and only Son? (He is God's one-of-a-kind Savior who is both man and God. There will never be another person who can do what He did on the cross.)

What does it mean to believe in Jesus? (To accept that Jesus died for your sins. When you trust that what God says about His death is true, you recognize your own wrongdoing and ask Him to enter and change your life, so you can give up sinning.)

What does this verse mean when it says you will not perish? (That you will have eternal life with God, even after death on this earth.)

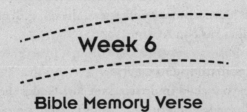

Week 6

Bible Memory Verse

For God sent not his Son into the world
to condemn the world; but that the world
through him might be saved.
John 3:17 KJV

"For God did not send his Son into the world
to condemn the world, but to save the
world through him."
John 3:17 NIV

"God sent his Son into the world not to judge
the world, but to save the world through him."
John 3:17 NLT

About This Verse

This verse helps us understand why Jesus came. It is heartening news that God wants to bring us into relationship with Him—not to condemn us. Those who see God as a stern judge have not understood the real goal of His sending His Son to earth.

Memorization Guideline

Help your child understand the love God is showing in this verse. God doesn't want to punish people but to bring them to Himself in love.

Learning Tips

This verse is a continuation of last week's. Review the previous verse before starting memorization this week.

Going Deeper

What does the word "condemn" mean? (To judge that someone's wrongdoing is worthy of the punishment of death).

What does it mean to be saved? (To be rescued from the death we justly deserve because of our sin).

What does this verse mean? (Jesus' purpose in coming to earth is not to judge us but to give us a loving relationship with God.)

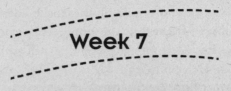

Week 7

Bible Memory Verse

He that believeth on him is not condemned:
but he that believeth not is condemned already,
because he hath not believed in the name
of the only begotten Son of God.
John 3:18 KJV

"Whoever believes in him is not condemned,
but whoever does not believe stands condemned
already because they have not believed in
the name of God's one and only Son."
John 3:18 NIV

"There is no judgment against anyone who
believes in him. But anyone who does not believe
in him has already been judged for not believing
in God's one and only Son."
John 3:18 NLT

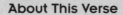

About This Verse

This verse continues the passages studied for the past two weeks. It shows how critical it is to make a decision for Christ—because that determines our eternal destination.

Memorization Guideline

This is a good opportunity to lead your child to Christ, if necessary, or to encourage your child to understand the importance of a decision already made. Has your child already believed in Jesus as Savior? How does that affect your child's life?

Learning Tips

This week completes a three-week memorization of John 3:16–18. Review both previous weeks before beginning memorization of this verse.

Going Deeper

Review what it means to be condemned—see last week's questions.

What is it that shows whether or not a person is condemned? (Believing—or not believing—in Jesus.)

What does it mean to believe in the "name" of Jesus? (To believe in who He really is. A name tells you what a person is really like. Just as your name is connected with your reputation, God's name tells you of His love and salvation. The name *Jesus* means "God saves."

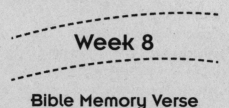

Week 8

Bible Memory Verse

Call unto me, and I will answer thee, and show thee
great and mighty things, which thou knowest not.
Jeremiah 33:3 KJV

"Call to me and I will answer you and tell you great
and unsearchable things you do not know."
Jeremiah 33:3 NIV

"Ask me and I will tell you remarkable secrets you do
not know about things to come."
Jeremiah 33:3 NLT

About This Verse

This is a powerful verse that helps us understand God's might. Though we are weak or limited, He is strong and all-knowing. He wants to share His knowledge with us.

Memorization Guideline

If you are memorizing with a young child, make this—as much as possible—a fun time. Encourage your child to read the verse with good expression or act out what's going on in the verse. If there is no fun in it, children find may scripture memorization drudgery.

Learning Tips

To review multiple verses, write each verse on paper or light cardboard. Each verse could be written in a different color. Cut the verses into separate words. Mix all the words together, then have your child put the pieces together into verses. Hold out the chapter and verse until the end, and let the child add each to the proper verse.

Going Deeper

What does God mean when He tells us to "call" on Him? (Your child can read the New Living Translation scripture and discover that it means we need to "ask" Him.)

Have you ever called out to God when things were really difficult and help was badly needed? What happened?

Did you realize God wants us to ask for His help? How does that make you feel about asking for His help?

What does this verse say God will do if you call on Him? (He will answer and show you great things). *Would you like to see these things?* (Encourage your child to look for the great things God will show to the believer.)

Week 9

Bible Memory Verse

For all have sinned, and come
short of the glory of God.
Romans 3:23 KJV

For all have sinned and fall
short of the glory of God.
Romans 3:23 NIV

For everyone has sinned;
we all fall short of God's glorious standard.
Romans 3:23 NLT

About This Verse

In a few simple words that even a child can understand, God makes it clear no one escapes the clutches of sin. None of us rise to God's perfect standard.

Memorization Guideline

A very short verse can be an important one. Help your child to take this verse seriously by emphasizing the power of sin to harm our lives and separate us from God. But remind your child that God has a solution for sin: Jesus.

Learning Tips

Using a Bible dictionary, look up the meaning of *glory*.

Going Deeper

What does this verse mean when it says "all" have sinned? (Every person has done wrong, and no one can claim to be perfect.)

What does it mean to "fall short of the glory of God" or "God's glorious standard"? (None of us can ever reach God's perfect holiness. We cannot always do the right thing.)

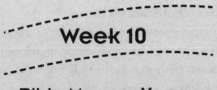

Week 10

Bible Memory Verse

If we say that we have no sin, we deceive
ourselves, and the truth is not in us.
1 John 1:8 KJV

If we claim to be without sin, we deceive
ourselves and the truth is not in us.
1 John 1:8 NIV

If we claim we have no sin, we are only fooling
ourselves and not living in the truth.
1 John 1:8 NLT

About This Verse

Humanity's great deception is to believe we don't sin. This verse directly confronts our belief that we never err or that our sins "aren't too bad." Sin is serious business.

Memorization Guideline

If your child resists this verse, it may be because some hidden sin makes the verse touch too close to home. Deal gently with that guilt, to bring your child into communion with God.

Learning Tips

Sometimes we don't like scripture's painful truths. If your child objects to this verse, discuss what the verse means and why your child is uncomfortable. Be gentle and loving in your interaction and pray that God will show your child the truth.

Going Deeper

How does this verse relate to Romans 3:23 from last week? (It is a response to people who do not believe they have sinned.)

What does this verse tell us about ourselves? (That we tend to fool ourselves about sin.)

How can we fool ourselves about our sin? (We think that the wrong we did isn't all that bad—or that we don't do anything wrong.)

Week 11

Bible Memory Verse

If we confess our sins, he is faithful
and just to forgive us our sins, and to
cleanse us from all unrighteousness.
1 John 1:9 KJV

If we confess our sins, he is faithful and
just and will forgive us our sins and purify
us from all unrighteousness.
1 John 1:9 NIV

But if we confess our sins to him,
he is faithful and just to forgive us our sins
and to cleanse us from all wickedness.
1 John 1:9 NLT

About This Verse

This verse describes part of God's solution for sin. Those who believe that Jesus died for their sins can unload them by confessing those sins to Him. When we really are sorry for our sins, He'll not only forgive us but will remove the stain of sin from our lives.

Memorization Guideline

The "if" in this verse is a big word. It's our natural response to hide from our sins instead of bringing them to God. Help your child understand that though it's difficult to admit wrongdoing, it is the only way to have peace with God.

Learning Tips

Review the verses from the past two weeks. Help your child see that Romans 3:23 tells of God's truth on the subject of sin, 1 John 1:8 is our reaction to being confronted with sin, and 1 John 1:9 is the solution to the problem. Remind your child that these verses are back-to-back by reading them together.

Going Deeper

Reread verse 1 John 1:8 and this week's verse.

How do we know that the truth is in us? (When we recognize our sin and confess it to God.)

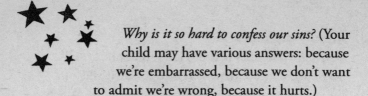

Why is it so hard to confess our sins? (Your child may have various answers: because we're embarrassed, because we don't want to admit we're wrong, because it hurts.)

Who is faithful? (God.) *Do we deserve His faithfulness?* (No, because we've been unfaithful by sinning.)

Is there any sin God cannot forgive? (No.) *How do we know that?* (Because He cleanses us from *all* unrighteousness.)

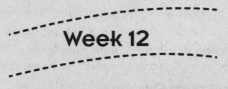

Week 12

Bible Memory Verse

Come now, and let us reason together,
saith the LORD: though your sins be as scarlet,
they shall be as white as snow; though they
be red like crimson, they shall be as wool.
Isaiah 1:18 KJV

"Come now, let us settle the matter," says the LORD.
"Though your sins are like scarlet, they shall be
as white as snow; though they are red as crimson,
they shall be like wool."
Isaiah 1:18 NIV

"Come now, let's settle this," says the LORD.
"Though your sins are like scarlet, I will make them
as white as snow. Though they are red like crimson,
I will make them as white as wool."
Isaiah 1:18 NLT

About This Verse

God pictures His power to cleanse sin by contrasting our scarlet and crimson-red sins to pure whiteness of snow and wool. Though we have been deeply colored by sin, God's forgiveness removes the stain completely.

Memorization Guideline

Children relate well to this kind of verbal picture of scriptural truth. Encourage your child to see what sin is like in this picture: A red stain (think of blood or a crimson dye) is one of the hardest to get out in the wash, yet God cleans us completely.

Learning Tips

Allow some time to discuss complex verses with your child. Memorization won't have much value if your child doesn't understand what a passage means.

Going Deeper

God promises He will make us white as snow when we ask His forgiveness.

Do you feel as white as snow, spiritually? What might it mean if you don't feel "white"? (That some sin is still between you and God.)

What do we need to do with that sin? (Confess it to God.)

What does this verse say about God? (That He can forgive sin and make our lives as clean as if the sin had never been there.)

Week 13

Bible Memory Verse

God is my strength and power:
and he maketh my way perfect.
2 Samuel 22:33 KJV

It is God who arms me with strength
and keeps my way secure.
2 Samuel 22:33 NIV

God is my strong fortress,
and he makes my way perfect.
2 Samuel 22:33 NLT

About This Verse

Under our own power, we often fail. Our lives can be filled with pain because of our inability to get things right. But when we rely on God to lead our lives, our ways fit His perfect plan—and we live in His perfect plan.

Memorization Guideline

This is another verse that pictures a truth about the relationship between God and us: We need His power to live perfect lives.

Learning Tips

What would it be like to have God's strength and power? Think about this before you begin memorization. You may want to look up *power* in a Bible dictionary.

Going Deeper

What does it mean to have God as your strength? (That we trust in Him to give us the strength to live in a way that pleases Him.)

How strong is God? (He is incredibly powerful. Share here some ideas you've gotten from your research in Learning Tips above.)

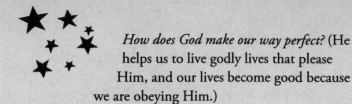

How does God make our way perfect? (He helps us to live godly lives that please Him, and our lives become good because we are obeying Him.)

Week 14

Bible Memory Verse

But they that wait upon the LORD shall renew their
strength; they shall mount up with wings as eagles;
they shall run, and not be weary;
and they shall walk, and not faint.
Isaiah 40:31 KJV

But those who hope in the LORD will renew their
strength. They will soar on wings like eagles;
they will run and not grow weary,
they will walk and not be faint.
Isaiah 40:31 NIV

But those who trust in the LORD will find new
strength. They will soar high on wings like eagles.
They will run and not grow weary.
They will walk and not faint.
Isaiah 40:31 NLT

About This Verse

Sometimes it's hard to wait for things to work out the way God has in mind. We want to rush off and do something—anything. But this verse reminds us that God often makes us wait. And when we do, God enables us to do even better things. When we wait for His timing, we will not fail.

Memorization Guideline

Make the most of the picture of eagles the Bible uses, describe those who soar in faith because they trust in God.

Learning Tips

If you have more than one child, have them help each other memorize longer verses. Write each verse on a card and have one child recite the verse while the other checks for accuracy. Allow hints for incorrect portions. Then have the children switch roles.

Going Deeper

Imagine an eagle, soaring in the air. It looks so effortless. This verse compares us to an eagle when we wait to do God's will.

What happens when we wait? (We find new strength.)

What is it like to be an eagle in God's plan? (Our lives go smoothly, like an eagle soaring on a wind current. We obey God easily.)

You do not have to run in order to do God's will. This verse describes those who trust in God as running and walking. How do we know which to do? (We must seek God's will for us and follow His timing.)

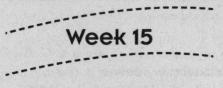

Week 15

Bible Memory Verse

And he said to them all, If any man will come after me, let him deny himself, and take up his cross daily, and follow me. For whosoever will save his life shall lose it: but whosoever will lose his life for my sake, the same shall save it.
Luke 9:23–24 KJV

Then he said to them all: "Whoever wants to be my disciple must deny themselves and take up their cross daily and follow me. For whoever wants to save their life will lose it, but whoever loses their life for me will save it."
Luke 9:23–24 NIV

Then he said to the crowd, "If any of you wants to be my follower, you must turn from your selfish ways, take up your cross daily, and follow me. If you try to hang on to your life, you will lose it. But if you give up your life for my sake, you will save it."
Luke 9:23–24 NLT

About These Verses
Living the Christian life is not always easy. Christians are called to deny themselves and do good for others as they follow the way of the cross.

Memorization Guideline
Not every verse in the Bible is "fun." This one describes a hard truth of the commitment it takes to be a Christian. But the end of the verse is a wonderful promise that our salvation is proved in these acts of selflessness.

Learning Tips
If it's helpful, allow younger children two weeks or more to memorize these verses.

Going Deeper
What does it mean to take up a cross? (Not to do what you want to but to do what God wants you to do.)

What does this verse mean when it says that whoever saves his life will lose it? (Those people who do not follow Jesus and do His will cannot have eternal life with God.)

What will happen if we give up our lives to God? (We will live with Him forever.)

Week 16

Bible Memory Verse

I am crucified with Christ: nevertheless I live; yet not
I, but Christ liveth in me: and the life which I now
live in the flesh I live by the faith of the Son of God,
who loved me, and gave himself for me.
Galatians 2:20 KJV

I have been crucified with Christ and I no longer live,
but Christ lives in me. The life I now live in the body,
I live by faith in the Son of God, who loved me
and gave himself for me.
Galatians 2:20 NIV

My old self has been crucified with Christ. It is no
longer I who live, but Christ lives in me. So I live in
this earthly body by trusting in the Son of God,
who loved me and gave himself for me.
Galatians 2:20 NLT

About This Verse

This verse is the apostle Paul's declaration concerning the way believers live the Christian life. No one can live faithfully in human power—but if we are "crucified with Christ," we can do God's will, appreciating the love it took for Him to die for us.

Memorization Guideline

Your child is deepening in relationship to God during memorization. Even when the words are jumbled and need more work, both of you can be encouraged. Don't focus so much on the actual words that your relationship is harmed. But make sure your child has a clear and accurate understanding of each verse.

Learning Tips

For longer verses, you may want to establish rewards when your child reaches a goal. Give a small treat or privilege for getting halfway through this verse.

Going Deeper

How can we be crucified with Christ, yet live? (We understand that our sins are wrong and it pains us deeply. We don't die physically, like Jesus, but we give up sin and fight our desire to sin.)

49

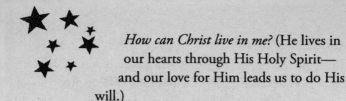 *How can Christ live in me?* (He lives in our hearts through His Holy Spirit— and our love for Him leads us to do His will.)

How can we live by faith in the Son of God? (We seek to obey Him every day of our lives.)

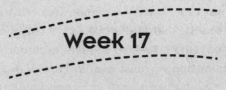

Week 17

Bible Memory Verse

For by grace are ye saved through faith;
and that not of yourselves: it is the gift of God:
Not of works, lest any man should boast.
Ephesians 2:8–9 KJV

For it is by grace you have been saved, through
faith—and this not from yourselves, it is the gift of
God—not by works, so that no one can boast.
Ephesians 2:8–9 NIV

God saved you by his grace when you believed. And
you can't take credit for this; it is a gift from God.
Salvation is not a reward for the good things we
have done, so none of us can boast about it.
Ephesians 2:8–9 NLT

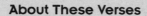

About These Verses

This is one of the most freeing passages in scripture. Our salvation does not depend on *us*, but on *God*, who gave salvation to us. We cannot work our way into faith, because that would make us in charge of our salvation. God graciously brought us into relationship with Him, and we must trust in Him alone.

Memorization Guideline

Look up *grace* in a Bible dictionary to help your child understand what it is. For a younger child, explain what you find there. Older children may want to do this research themselves.

Learning Tips

Find the best time to memorize for your family. If morning is too rushed, it may be better to memorize, for example, after dinner.

Going Deeper

What is grace? (Unmerited favor or a gift we could never have earned.)

How do we get grace? (God gives it to us as a gift.)

Why doesn't God let us earn our salvation? (So we can't boast about our own works that caused us to know Him.)

Have you accepted God's gift of salvation?

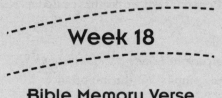

Week 18

Bible Memory Verse

That if thou shalt confess with thy mouth the Lord Jesus, and shalt believe in thine heart that God hath raised him from the dead, thou shalt be saved. For with the heart man believeth unto righteousness; and with the mouth confession is made unto salvation.
Romans 10:9–10 KJV

If you declare with your mouth, "Jesus is Lord," and believe in your heart that God raised him from the dead, you will be saved. For it is with your heart that you believe and are justified, and it is with your mouth that you profess your faith and are saved.
Romans 10:9–10 NIV

If you confess with your mouth that Jesus is Lord and believe in your heart that God raised him from the dead, you will be saved. For it is by believing in your heart that you are made right with God, and it is by confessing with your mouth that you are saved.
Romans 10:9–10 NLT

About These Verses

What does it take to be saved? Paul describes the connection between *saying* you're a Christian and *believing* it. Faith takes both. The parallel construction here, in which Paul repeats and reverses the ideas, emphasizes the importance of both.

Memorization Guideline

If your child prays at bedtime, that's a good time to review the verse for the day or remember a previous verse.

Learning Tips

Younger children may take two weeks or more to memorize these verses. Begin the second week by reviewing the first verse.

Going Deeper

In this verse, what does it mean to confess? (To openly tell of your faith.) Help your child understand that this does not necessarily mean you need to confront the school bully with your faith—but that you should be ready to tell others of what you believe about Jesus.

What does it mean to say "Jesus is Lord"? (That Jesus is in charge of your life and you will follow Him.)

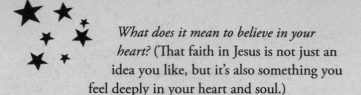

What does it mean to believe in your heart? (That faith in Jesus is not just an idea you like, but it's also something you feel deeply in your heart and soul.)

Week 19

Bible Memory Verse

Verily, verily, I say unto you, He that heareth
my word, and believeth on him that sent me,
hath everlasting life, and shall not come into
condemnation; but is passed from death unto life.
John 5:24 KJV

"Very truly I tell you, whoever hears my word and
believes him who sent me has eternal life and will not
be judged but has crossed over from death to life."
John 5:24 NIV

"I tell you the truth, those who listen to my message
and believe in God who sent me have eternal life.
They will never be condemned for their sins, but they
have already passed from death into life."
John 5:24 NLT

About This Verse

God's Word, the Bible, is an important part of Christianity, because it provides us with God's truth. Through scripture, we come to know our Lord. When we hear God's words to us, we can come to faith in Him and be saved.

Memorization Guideline

Help your child to understand the importance of the Bible in the Christian life. Through its message, we come to faith, live daily in faith, and have faith to believe in God's coming kingdom.

Learning Tips

If you're using the King James Version, you may wish to use the more modern verses to help your child understand unfamiliar words. For example, *verily* is an older word for "truly."

Going Deeper

What does this verse say we have to do? (Listen and believe.)

How important is listening to know God's message for us? (Very important. We need to hear His message to believe.)

Rate your own listening skills. Are you: a) barely listening, b) listening some of the time, c) listening as much as possible? How can you improve your listening? (Through paying attention when you read the Bible and taking it seriously.)

What does listening and believing result in? (Our having eternal life.)

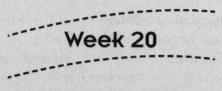

Week 20

Bible Memory Verse

There is therefore now no condemnation to them
which are in Christ Jesus, who walk not after the
flesh, but after the Spirit.
Romans 8:1 KJV

Therefore, there is now no condemnation for those
who are in Christ Jesus.
Romans 8:1 NIV

So now there is no condemnation for those who
belong to Christ Jesus.
Romans 8:1 NLT

About This Verse
This verse describes more of the freedom we have when we believe in Christ and follow Him. We do not need to fear God, because He has saved us from all sin.

Memorization Guideline
Make sure your child understands what "condemnation" means. When God condemns someone, He says that person is guilty of sin against God. Those who are guilty have not experienced God's salvation—it is salvation which makes God their loving Father. Though God created all people, only those who believe in Jesus are truly His children, able to experience all His love.

Learning Tips
Help your child understand that this verse is not designed to make believers feel guilty, but to make them experience the freedom that obedience to God brings.

Going Deeper
What does "condemnation" mean? (A judgment that one is guilty of wrongdoing.)

Why doesn't God condemn us? (Because we believe in Jesus.)

What does it mean to walk after the Spirit, or be in Christ Jesus? (To have believed that He died for your sins and that you need to follow Him throughout your life by doing what He wants you to do.)

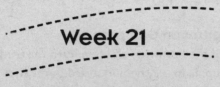

Week 21

Bible Memory Verse

Trust in the LORD with all thine heart;
and lean not unto thine own understanding.
Proverbs 3:5 KJV

Trust in the LORD with all your heart and
lean not on your own understanding.
Proverbs 3:5 NIV

Trust in the LORD with all your heart;
do not depend on your own understanding.
Proverbs 3:5 NLT

About This Verse

This verse teaches us how to live well—by teaching us we cannot trust in our own flawed judgment and abilities. When we trust in God completely, our lives fall in line with His will, and we live in peace.

Memorization Guideline

One of the best ways children learn the truths of scripture is to see them modeled in the lives of other Christians. Are you living out this verse so that your child can see what it means to trust daily in God?

Learning Tips

This verse and Proverbs 3:6 (next week's scripture) are back-to-back in the Bible and may be memorized together, in the same week, if your child is capable.

Going Deeper

What does it mean to "lean" on your own understanding? (To trust in your own decisions and wisdom, without consulting God.) *Isn't this a good picture of how we depend on our own minds and intelligence?*

How can we trust in the Lord instead? (By reading and memorizing scripture, praying, asking His will in all we do, and putting Him first in our lives and choices.)

Week 22

Bible Memory Verse

In all thy ways acknowledge him,
and he shall direct thy paths.
Proverbs 3:6 KJV

In all your ways submit to him,
and he will make your paths straight.
Proverbs 3:6 NIV

Seek his will in all you do, and he
will show you which path to take.
Proverbs 3:6 NLT

About This Verse

This verse, coupled with last week's, gives us an idea of what's really important in our lives. Are we centered on Him or other things? These back-to-back verses show us where our trust should be.

Memorization Guideline

Remind your child that this verse immediately follows the one memorized last week. Begin by reviewing that verse.

Learning Tips

Don't try to cram too much learning into one time period. If your child is having trouble memorizing, work for short times, on a few words at a time, throughout one day.

Going Deeper

Who is the "he" that's spoken of in this verse? (Clue: The answer is in last week's verse. "He" is the Lord.)

What does it mean to "acknowledge" God? How do you do that in your life? (Acknowledging God is not just admitting He is there, but making Him part of every moment of your life.)

How do we know what path God wants us to walk on?
(By studying His Word, so we know what is right,
and praying for His guidance.)

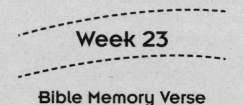

Week 23

Bible Memory Verse

Blessed are they which do hunger and thirst after
righteousness: for they shall be filled.
Matthew 5:6 KJV

"Blessed are those who hunger and thirst for
righteousness, for they will be filled."
Matthew 5:6 NIV

"God blesses those who hunger and thirst for justice,
for they will be satisfied."
Matthew 5:6 NLT

About This Verse

Those who deeply desire to live in God's right ways (in His righteousness) receive a spiritual filling that draws them ever closer to God. The world will never show that to us. But reading God's Word, being part of a faithful church, and seeking God in prayer fuel our hunger for Him—and fill that hunger. As we seek God, He gives us great blessings.

Memorization Guideline

Using a Bible dictionary, look up the word *righteous*. Help your child understand that righteousness is a lifestyle, not just an occasional thing. When we live in God's ways, we draw closer to Him and are blessed in our everyday lives.

Learning Tips

Don't just focus on individual words as your child memorizes. Keep the meaning of the whole verse in mind, so its sense is not lost.

Going Deeper

What does it mean to hunger and thirst for righteousness? (To desire it deeply.) *Have you felt this desire to know God better?*

Why would God bless those who hunger and thirst for Him? (Because they want to know Him better and are doing His will.)

 *What does it mean to be filled?* (To be spiritually satisfied with a deep relationship with God.)

Week 24

Bible Memory Verse

Thy word is a lamp unto my feet,
and a light unto my path.
Psalm 119:105 KJV

Your word is a lamp for my feet,
a light on my path.
Psalm 119:105 NIV

Your word is a lamp to guide my feet
and a light for my path.
Psalm 119:105 NLT

About This Verse

The psalmist compares God's Word to a lamp that guides the Christian pilgrim on the right path. No matter what we face in life, scripture guides us in how we should act.

Memorization Guideline

This verse may be more meaningful if your child learns about the kind of lamps that were used during the Old Testament period. The kind of lamp in this verse was small, able to be held in one hand, and burned oil. It would allow a person to see a short distance ahead. God is saying that He gives enough light for today's travels—though not necessarily a bright light to illuminate our lives miles ahead. This is what it means to "walk in faith."

Learning Tips

Look up the word *lamp* in an illustrated Bible dictionary to see the kind of lamps the psalmist refers to.

Going Deeper

With these words, God is drawing a picture of what it's like to follow Him.

What does it mean when He tells us that His Word is a lamp to our feet? (That every day He gives us enough light to guide us in the right direction.)

Can you trust God to give you enough light to see where you are going today? (Yes.)

If you cannot see farther than today, is that okay? Why? (Yes, because tomorrow He will give light for that day, too.)

73

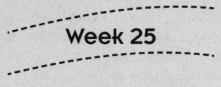

Week 25

Bible Memory Verse

For the word of God is quick, and powerful, and sharper than any twoedged sword, piercing even to the dividing asunder of soul and spirit, and of the joints and marrow, and is a discerner of the thoughts and intents of the heart.
Hebrews 4:12 KJV

For the word of God is alive and active. Sharper than any double-edged sword, it penetrates even to dividing soul and spirit, joints and marrow; it judges the thoughts and attitudes of the heart.
Hebrews 4:12 NIV

For the word of God is alive and powerful. It is sharper than the sharpest two-edged sword, cutting between soul and spirit, between joint and marrow. It exposes our innermost thoughts and desires.
Hebrews 4:12 NLT

About This Verse

When the author of Hebrews describes God's Word, he uses an illustration of a common offensive weapon of that day. The Roman two-edged sword had cutting surfaces on each side, allowing a soldier to thrust into his opponent deeply. Just like that sharp sword, God's Word cuts deeply into our lives and makes us aware of our sins.

Memorization Guideline

Make sure your child understands what joints and marrow are. This passage describes the innermost parts of our bones. It is a picture of how God's Word cuts into every part of a human being, even the most hidden places.

If you are using the King James Version, explain to your child that *quick* meant "alive" in that day.

Learning Tips

Younger children may take two weeks or more to memorize this verse.

Going Deeper

What does the Bible mean when it describes the Word as being alive? (It is not just words on a page. Because God's Spirit applies scripture to our lives, it has a life of its own that influences us.)

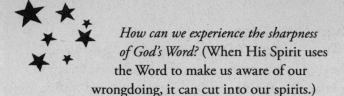

How can we experience the sharpness of God's Word? (When His Spirit uses the Word to make us aware of our wrongdoing, it can cut into our spirits.)

Name two things this verse says the sword of the Word does. (It pierces—penetrates or cuts—and it discerns—judges or exposes—our thoughts and attitudes).

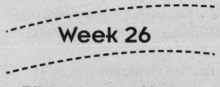

Week 26

Bible Memory Verse

Every word of God is pure: he is a shield
unto them that put their trust in him.
Proverbs 30:5 KJV

"Every word of God is flawless; he is a shield
to those who take refuge in him."
Proverbs 30:5 NIV

Every word of God proves true. He is a shield
to all who come to him for protection.
Proverbs 30:5 NLT

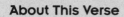

About This Verse

This Bible verse helps us trust in everything God says. The various versions have different ways of translating it—"pure," "flawless," and "proves true." Any way you slice it, God's Word can be relied on. There is no error in it. Not only that, it is protection for those who believe that truth.

Memorization Guideline

When God tells us He will protect us, we can trust Him. That's why the first part of this verse is so important. If whatever God says is true, and He says He will be our protection, we can trust that that will happen. Help your child put trust in God, knowing He will never fail.

Learning Tips

Encourage your child to see God as a shield. As Christians, we can turn to Him and ask for protection.

Going Deeper

When the Bible tells us God's word is pure, flawless, or true, what it is saying? (That we can trust everything He says.)

What does a shield do for a soldier? (It protects him from his enemy.)

What is God saying when He talks about shielding believers? (He will stand between us and our enemies.) *Who is our main enemy?* (Satan.)

What do we have to do to get that protection? (Trust in God.) *Have you ever asked God for protection?*

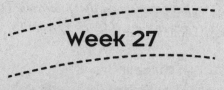

Week 27

Bible Memory Verse

Study to shew thyself approved unto God,
a workman that needeth not to be ashamed,
rightly dividing the word of truth.
2 Timothy 2:15 KJV

Do your best to present yourself to God as one
approved, a worker who does not need to be ashamed
and who correctly handles the word of truth.
2 Timothy 2:15 NIV

Work hard so you can present yourself to God
and receive his approval. Be a good worker,
one who does not need to be ashamed and
who correctly explains the word of truth.
2 Timothy 2:15 NLT

About This Verse

The apostle Paul wrote these words as advice to Timothy. What was true for this young church leader is also true for us. How we deal with God's Word is important because it is the basis of our testimony to what He has done in our lives.

Memorization Guideline

Does your child understand the importance of scripture in the Christian life? You might share a time when a Bible verse was helpful in your life, perhaps in making a decision, keeping you from sin, or encouraging you.

Learning Tips

To help with memorization, have your child write the verses or type them into a computer each day.

Going Deeper

Have you ever thought that you are God's worker? What kind of work do you do for Him? (Tell people about Him. Show them what it is like to be a Christian.)

How can you gain God's approval? (By learning His Word, obeying Him, and sharing Bible truths with others.)

How can you correctly explain the word of truth? (By knowing what His Word means and sharing it with others.)

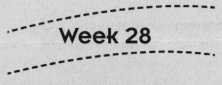

Week 28

Bible Memory Verse

The fear of the LORD is the beginning of knowledge:
but fools despise wisdom and instruction.
Proverbs 1:7 KJV

The fear of the LORD is the beginning of knowledge,
but fools despise wisdom and instruction.
Proverbs 1:7 NIV

Fear of the LORD is the foundation of true knowledge,
but fools despise wisdom and discipline.
Proverbs 1:7 NLT

About This Verse

When people truly believe in God (or "fear" Him), they understand things they never knew before. Those who turn from Him, however, despise the wisdom and instruction He offers.

Memorization Guideline

Be certain your child knows that biblical fear doesn't mean believers cower in anticipation of God doing something bad to them. "Fear" means that we respect God, as we would respect a parent or other authority figure. But since God is so much greater than earthly authority figures, He commands even more respect than they do.

Learning Tips

Help your child seek God's wisdom by learning more about Him. Encourage Christian disciplines such as Bible study, prayer, and church attendance.

Going Deeper

If we fear (or respect) God, how will we act and think? (As if He is important. We will want to spend time with Him and obey Him.)

How will we act if we despise Him? (We will avoid Him, His Word, and faith in Him.)

How is knowledge connected to fear of God? (When we fear Him, we will learn about Him and follow His ways.)

Why are people fools not to believe in God? (Because He is so powerful and can lead them to salvation. Not to believe in Him means they will not be with Him in eternity.)

Week 29

Bible Memory Verse

Finally, my brethren, be strong in the Lord, and in the power of his might. Put on the whole armour of God, that ye may be able to stand against the wiles of the devil.
Ephesians 6:10–11 KJV

Finally, be strong in the Lord and in his mighty power. Put on the full armor of God so that you can take your stand against the devil's schemes.
Ephesians 6:10–11 NIV

A final word: Be strong in the Lord and in his mighty power. Put on all of God's armor so that you will be able to stand firm against all strategies of the devil.
Ephesians 6:10–11 NLT

About These Verses

This is the beginning of Paul's description of God's armor, the protective "suit" that shields the believer from Satan's temptations. Verses 13–17 describe each part of the armor.

Memorization Guideline

Help your child understand that, as Christians, our power comes from God. But we are responsible for resisting temptation by putting on the armor Paul describes in the following verses.

Learning Tips

Older children may also memorize the *reason* we need God's armor and its parts, described in Ephesians 6:12–17. The armor Paul describes here is what a Roman soldier would have worn. In a Bible dictionary, see if you can find a picture of the armor he's describing and share it with your child. Read verses 6:12–17 to younger children, so they understand this verse.

Going Deeper

Where do we, as Christians, get our ability to faithfully follow God? (From Him, because we are to be strong in the Lord and His power.)

God gives us a picture of His protection against the devil. What does He call it? (Armor.)

What does it help us do? (Stand up against Satan's temptations.)

Week 30

Bible Memory Verse

But without faith it is impossible to please him: for he
that cometh to God must believe that he is, and that
he is a rewarder of them that diligently seek him.
Hebrews 11:6 KJV

And without faith it is impossible to please God,
because anyone who comes to him must believe
that he exists and that he rewards those
who earnestly seek him.
Hebrews 11:6 NIV

And it is impossible to please God without faith.
Anyone who wants to come to him must believe
that God exists and that he rewards those
who sincerely seek him.
Hebrews 11:6 NLT

About This Verse

This verse is found in the description of the faith of the Old Testament heroes outlined in Hebrews 11. But these words are also critical to *our* walk in the Spirit, for faith is the starting point of any relationship with God.

Memorization Guideline

This verse is not mere spiritual theory. Every person who claims the name of Jesus must implicitly trust in Him and believe that He purposes good for those with such trust. Encourage your children to apply these words to their own lives.

Learning Tips

If your child gets antsy, making learning difficult, try a few exercises to expend that energy. Do them together—then return to the work of memorization.

Going Deeper

What do we have to have in order to please God? (Faith.)

Why? (Because we must believe He exists and rewards people in order to trust Him.)

Would you believe in God if you didn't know that He was real and would do good things for you? (No.)

What does it mean to "earnestly," "sincerely," or "diligently" seek God? (To really believe in Him and obey Him.)

Week 31

Bible Memory Verse

I can do all things through Christ
which strengtheneth me.
Philippians 4:13 KJV

I can do all this through him who gives me strength.
Philippians 4:13 NIV

For I can do everything through Christ,
who gives me strength.
Philippians 4:13 NLT

About This Verse

Scripture often speaks of God giving us strength. Whatever your child needs to do in life, God can provide the strength for it. God wants to give His children the ability to live powerful Christian lives. We need only to lean on Him and ask Him for help.

Memorization Guideline

If God does not give your child strength to do something, perhaps it's something He does not have in mind for your child. Even good things are sometimes not part of God's will for us. But for anything that is in God's plan for a Christian, God will give strength.

Learning Tips

Do not forget to review verses you have worked on in previous weeks. Continual repetition will keep them in your child's mind. This is a good week for review, since the verse is short.

Going Deeper

As Christians, what do we need God's strength for? (To do anything He asks us to do, whether it is avoiding sin or doing good works.)

 *Why do we need His strength?* (Because under our own power, we cannot resist sin and do the good things we can do in Him.)

What would you like to have God's strength to do? Have you asked Him for it?

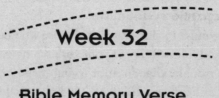

Week 32

Bible Memory Verse

Many are the afflictions of the righteous:
but the Lord delivereth him out of them all.
Psalm 34:19 KJV

The righteous person may have many troubles,
but the Lord delivers him from them all.
Psalm 34:19 NIV

The righteous person faces many troubles,
but the Lord comes to the rescue each time.
Psalm 34:19 NLT

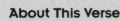

About This Verse

This is a verse of great comfort to believers who are going through trials. God is faithful to rescue those who trust in Him.

Memorization Guideline

The promise in this verse is for those who believe in God and follow Him. If your children have questions about troubles that an unbelieving friend or family member has faced, let them know that Psalm 34:19 is not a blanket promise for everyone. Both unbelievers and Christians face troubles—only believers can rely on God for the solution.

Learning Tips

Encourage a child who is beginning to remember parts of the verse but does not have it down pat yet. Don't criticize. Then continue to work on the verse until it is word-perfect.

Going Deeper

What are afflictions? (Troubles.)

What does it mean to be "righteous"? (To be right with God by knowing and following Him.)

When God delivers us, does it mean we always land in the most pleasant situation? (Not necessarily. But God will always do what is best for us.)

Will God always be faithful to rescue us? (Yes, though perhaps not in the way we expected.)

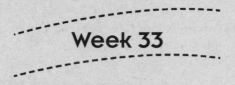

Week 33

Bible Memory Verse

God is our refuge and strength, a very present
help in trouble. Therefore will not we fear, though
the earth be removed, and though the mountains
be carried into the midst of the sea.
Psalm 46:1–2 KJV

God is our refuge and strength, an ever-present
help in trouble. Therefore we will not fear,
though the earth give way and the mountains
fall into the heart of the sea.
Psalm 46:1–2 NIV

God is our refuge and strength, always ready
to help in times of trouble. So we will not
fear when earthquakes come and the
mountains crumble into the sea.
Psalm 46:1–2 NLT

About These Verses

This passage encourages believers to take refuge in God, no matter what happens. Even if the whole world is destroyed, God will be with us, helping us. He will never desert us.

Memorization Guideline

Focus on the word-pictures of this passage to help your child memorize it. Many picturesque words in these verses will help your child remember the action of the verses. Your child may even want to draw a picture of these verses.

Learning Tips

For younger children or children who have a hard time memorizing, you may split these verses over two weeks.

Going Deeper

What is a refuge? (A place you go to for protection.)

What does it mean when this verse says God is "a very present" or "ever-present" help in trouble? (That He is always near us in trouble and ready to help.)

Is there ever a time when God does not want to help us? (No.)

Why might it seem that He's not helping us? (If we do not turn to Him for help or if He knows it will be best for the help to come at another time.)

If our help does not come right away, what should we do? (Wait and trust God.)

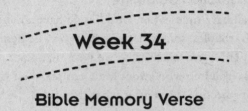

Week 34

Bible Memory Verse

I will say of the LORD, He is my refuge and my
fortress: my God; in him will I trust.
Psalm 91:2 KJV

I will say of the LORD, "He is my refuge and my
fortress, my God, in whom I trust."
Psalm 91:2 NIV

This I declare about the LORD: He alone is my refuge,
my place of safety; he is my God, and I trust him.
Psalm 91:2 NLT

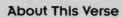

About This Verse

This verse creates a picture of trusting in God: It's like taking refuge in a fortress, when your enemy is about to attack.

Memorization Guideline

We all have times when we'd like to have a refuge from troubles, somewhere we can go to be perfectly safe. This verse tells us that we have that place in God. Children who know Jesus can put their trust in His protection, no matter what they face.

Learning Tips

If your child has had a hard day, you may want to simply read the verse together a few times. Tired minds do not memorize well. You can save serious memory work for a time when your child feels sharper. Repetition is one easy way of getting a verse into your child's brain.

Going Deeper

What would it be like, when an enemy was about to attack, to go into a fortress? (It might be a frightening time—but you would know you would be safe in the fortress.)

How is God like a fortress? (He provides safety from sin for those who trust in Him.)

Do you feel safe with Him?

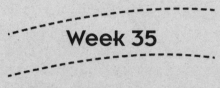

Week 35

Bible Memory Verse

I will call upon the LORD, who is worthy to be
praised: so shall I be saved from mine enemies.
Psalm 18:3 KJV

I called to the LORD, who is worthy of praise,
and I have been saved from my enemies.
Psalm 18:3 NIV

I called on the LORD, who is worthy of praise,
and he saved me from my enemies.
Psalm 18:3 NLT

About This Verse
Last week we learned how God protects us. Here we learn about our part in dealing with enemies: We must call on God and ask for help.

Memorization Guideline
The psalmist can confidently say that God is worthy to be praised because he has experience with God. God has been there for the psalmist before—and God will be there for him again. Help your child remember times when God has helped your family, trusting that He will always be there.

Learning Tips
Memorization requires a time commitment. Make certain you and your child set aside enough time to do the job properly instead of hurrying through a verse for a minute or two.

Going Deeper
How do we call on God? (Through prayer.)

Do you regularly pray for God's help? If not, why not? How can you change that?

Does God want us to call on Him just once? (No, He wants us to constantly call on Him.)

What does He promise to do for us in this verse? (Save us from our enemies.)

What enemies do we face every day? (Temptations to sin.)

Do we need His help every day in that? (Yes.)

Week 36

Bible Memory Verse

Casting all your care upon him;
for he careth for you.
1 Peter 5:7 KJV

Cast all your anxiety on him
because he cares for you.
1 Peter 5:7 NIV

Give all your worries and cares to God,
for he cares about you.
1 Peter 5:7 NLT

About This Verse

Just as God called the leaders of the first-century church to depend on Him, He wants us to turn to Him with all our cares. There is no concern of ours that is not God's concern, too.

Memorization Guideline

Though children have different cares than adults, their concerns are still important to God. Youngsters may worry about how they'll do on a test at school or about what a friend thinks of them—and these issues are important parts of their mental and social development. God wants to help them in what may seem to adults as small concerns.

Learning Tips

If your child is having trouble accepting that God cares about even the small things in a child's life, read Matthew 10:29–31 together. If God can care about those little sparrows, won't He care for your child?

Going Deeper

How do we give our cares—or anxiety or worries—to God? (By praying to Him and asking for help.)

How can we know He has heard our prayers? (Because He promises to.)

If we do not immediately get an answer to our prayers, does that mean God is not listening? (No.)

What can it mean? (That He will still answer, if we continue to trust in Him.)

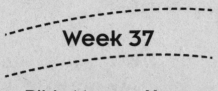

Week 37

Bible Memory Verse

And we know that all things work together for good to them that love God, to them who are the called according to his purpose.
Romans 8:28 KJV

And we know that in all things God works for the good of those who love him, who have been called according to his purpose.
Romans 8:28 NIV

And we know that God causes everything to work together for the good of those who love God and are called according to his purpose for them.
Romans 8:28 NLT

About This Verse

When we face many challenges, life can seem a terrible mess. But when we love God and seek to do His will, we can trust He will bring us many blessings.

Memorization Guideline

Those who love God are the ones whom He has "called according to His purpose." So we can trust that whatever we face in life, whether it's pleasurable or testing, He is working it together for our good.

Learning Tips

If your child is facing challenges today, use this verse as a reminder that God always loves His children and will help with those troubles. This is a good verse to repeat over and over, either mentally or out loud, to keep that encouragement alive.

Going Deeper

This verse promises that everything will work together for good.

For Christians, does that mean life will always be extremely happy? (No.)

What does it mean? (That in the end, whatever we go through will benefit us.)

111

Who are "the called according to his purpose"? (Those who love God, who believe in Him.)

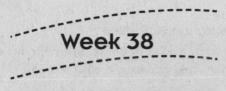

Week 38

Bible Memory Verse

Blessed is the man that walketh not in the counsel
of the ungodly, nor standeth in the way of sinners,
nor sitteth in the seat of the scornful.
Psalm 1:1 KJV

Blessed is the one who does not walk in step with
the wicked or stand in the way that sinners take
or sit in the company of mockers.
Psalm 1:1 NIV

Oh, the joys of those who do not follow
the advice of the wicked, or stand around
with sinners, or join in with mockers.
Psalm 1:1 NLT

About This Verse
To be "blessed" means to have God's favor. The scriptures often connect God's blessing with obedience.

Memorization Guideline
If you need to, look *blessed* up in a Bible dictionary to help your child understand what it means.

Learning Tips
Next week your child will memorize the next verse, Psalm 1:2, which will give a more complete picture of what it means to be blessed.

Going Deeper
What does it means to be blessed? (To have God's favor or approval.)

Is this verse saying that only men can get God's approval? (No, "man" is another way of saying "people" in the Bible.)

Who are these blessed people? (Those who love and follow God.)

Name three things the blessed person does not do. (Follow the advice of wicked or ungodly people, stand with sinners, or sit with mockers—or the scornful).

What do these expressions mean? (That the blessed person will not make such people their close friends and take advice from them.)

Week 39

Bible Memory Verse

But his delight is in the law of the Lord;
and in his law doth he meditate day and night.
Psalm 1:2 KJV

But whose delight is in the law of the Lord,
and who meditates on his law day and night.
Psalm 1:2 NIV

But they delight in the law of the Lord,
meditating on it day and night.
Psalm 1:2 NLT

About This Verse

Last week we studied what a blessed person does *not* do. In this second verse of Psalm 1, we see how the Christian *should* live—making the Bible and its teachings the focus of every thought.

Memorization Guideline

This is a continuation of last week's verse. Review last week's verse and combine the two this week.

Learning Tips

You may also have your child memorize Psalm 1:3, which completes the description of the blessed person. Or you may work on memorizing the entire psalm, which is only six verses long. The latter portion of Psalm 1 describes the judgment God has in store for those who do not follow Him.

Going Deeper

What does it mean to delight in the law? (To enjoy it and want to read and understand it.)

Who delights in the law? (Those who know God and want to obey Him.)

What does it mean to "meditate"? (To think deeply and ponder.)

Why does God tell us to do this? (By meditating on His Word, we can make God the center of our life.)

Week 40

Bible Memory Verse

And all things, whatsoever ye shall ask
in prayer, believing, ye shall receive.
Matthew 21:22 KJV

"If you believe, you will receive
whatever you ask for in prayer."
Matthew 21:22 NIV

"You can pray for anything, and if
you have faith, you will receive it."
Matthew 21:22 NLT

About This Verse

Could there be a greater encouragement to prayer than this verse? God wants us to ask Him for whatever we need. We need not fear that He will meanly deny us. But we should also ask wisely for the things He says are best for us. And we need to ask with faith that He will provide.

Memorization Guideline

This verse does not encourage your child to ask for an unending array of toys or electronics. God will not give things that are bad for us. But it does encourage believers to ask about real needs that are within His will for us—and He will provide.

Learning Tips

Help your child identify real physical and spiritual needs and bring them to God in prayer. You may want to end this memory session in prayer. Remember that your prayer can be an example to your child in how to pray faithfully.

Going Deeper

Is there anything you cannot ask God for? (No.)

If your prayer is not in His will for you, how will He answer? ("No.")

If it's not something He wants you to have now, how may He answer? (Wait.)

What else could keep God from answering? (Unbelief on our part.)

If we ask something that's in God's will and believe, will He answer? (Yes, though His answer is sometimes different from the one we expected.)

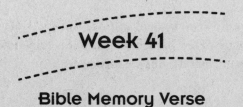

Week 41

Bible Memory Verse

Know ye not that ye are the temple of God,
and that the Spirit of God dwelleth in you?
1 Corinthians 3:16 KJV

Don't you know that you yourselves are God's temple
and that God's Spirit dwells in your midst?
1 Corinthians 3:16 NIV

Don't you realize that all of you together
are the temple of God and that the
Spirit of God lives in you?
1 Corinthians 3:16 NLT

About This Verse

God has chosen to be with His people as the Holy Spirit lives in their hearts. Paul compares this to the Old Testament temple, where God dwelt with His people. How much more wonderful is it that He lives today in every Christian?

Memorization Guideline

It's important for your child to understand what an honor it is to have God living within. It can make a child more aware of how important all people are to God.

Learning Tips

Use an illustrated Bible dictionary to show young children what God's temple looked like. Point out that it was here God was worshipped and sacrifices were made to Him. Now, when there is no temple, God lives inside His people, through His Spirit, who is in their hearts.

Going Deeper

Is anyone who is His temple important to God? (Yes.)

Why? (Because He makes His home in them.)

Knowing that, how should we treat other Christians? (As if they are important, because God says they are.)

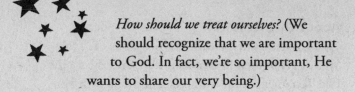

How should we treat ourselves? (We should recognize that we are important to God. In fact, we're so important, He wants to share our very being.)

What happened in the temple? (Sacrifice and worship.)

What did it mean to people's faith? (It helped them understand God and His forgiveness.)

How was it different from faith today? (There are now no temple or sacrifices. Jesus is our sacrifice.)

How was it the same? (We worship the same God.)

Discuss how Christians should live, knowing that they are God's temple. Have your child look up 1 Corinthians 3:17 to see how seriously God considers a person being His temple.

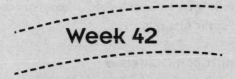

Week 42

Bible Memory Verse

A new commandment I give unto you,
That ye love one another; as I have loved you,
that ye also love one another.
John 13:34 KJV

"A new command I give you: Love one another.
As I have loved you, so you must love one another."
John 13:34 NIV

"So now I am giving you a new commandment:
Love each other. Just as I have loved you,
you should love each other."
John 13:34 NLT

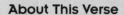

About This Verse

Before His crucifixion, Jesus gave this commandment to His twelve closest disciples. Jesus knew love would help His church stay together when He was no longer physically present. That love is as important today as it was in the first century.

Memorization Guideline

Recognize that loving others can be difficult for your child. It's been a challenge to every believer down through the ages, especially when faced with enemies or dissension in the church. Sometimes love is a decision. Only through Jesus can we find this kind of love.

Learning Tips

The kind of love Jesus talks about here is not just a touchy-feely kind. The Greek word used here is *agape* (pronounced ah-GAH-pay), which means "divine love." God is calling us to love others in the same way He loves us—unselfishly. Encourage your child to talk about how hard it can be to love and the challenge of choosing to love even when it may be difficult.

Going Deeper

In three words, sum up the commandment Jesus gave His disciples. (Love one another.)

Who is to be our example in love? (Jesus.)

How was He an example? (He loved us enough to die for us.)

Is loving other people easy for you? Hard? Why? (Encourage your child to understand that sometimes love comes to us easily, but many times it can be a sacrifice of obedience to Jesus.)

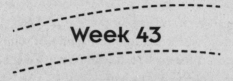

Week 43

Bible Memory Verse

Beloved, let us love one another:
for love is of God; and every one that loveth
is born of God, and knoweth God.
1 John 4:7 KJV

Dear friends, let us love one another,
for love comes from God. Everyone who loves
has been born of God and knows God.
1 John 4:7 NIV

Dear friends, let us continue to love one another,
for love comes from God. Anyone who loves
is a child of God and knows God.
1 John 4:7 NLT

About This Verse

Last week your child memorized John 13:34, in which Jesus commanded us to love one another. This verse expands our knowledge of the relationship between love and God. Love is so interconnected with God that to love Him is to love others, too.

Memorization Guideline

The word for "love" in this verse is the Greek word *agape* (pronounced ah-GAH-pay), which means "divine love." We cannot truly love others the way God does without His enabling power.

Learning Tips

At the appropriate point below, review last week's verse, which also deals with love and God.

Going Deeper

Why should we love one another? (Because love is of God—it comes from God.)

What did Jesus say about loving one another in last week's verse? (He commanded us to love one another.)

For you, does this settle the need to love others, even when it isn't easy?

What does loving others show about us?
(That we love God.)

When we have trouble loving others, how can we do it? (By asking Him to help us to love, because love comes from Him.)

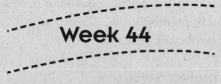

Week 44

Bible Memory Verse

Honour thy father and thy mother:
that thy days may be long upon the land
which the LORD thy God giveth thee.
Exodus 20:12 KJV

"Honor your father and your mother,
so that you may live long in the land
the LORD your God is giving you."
Exodus 20:12 NIV

"Honor your father and mother.
Then you will live a long, full life in the
land the LORD your God is giving you."
Exodus 20:12 NLT

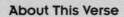

About This Verse

This verse, which is one of the Ten Commandments, is called the first commandment with a promise. Here God promises that those who honor their parents will live long in His promised land. There is often a practical benefit to obeying God.

Memorization Guideline

Though this verse was particularly aimed at God's people who were receiving the Law, the apostle Paul reaffirms its truths in Ephesians 6:1–3.

Learning Tips

As your child's parent, you may have to go a bit lightly on this verse. Demanding obedience is often less successful than allowing a child to hear God's Word and allowing Him to use it in your child's life.

Going Deeper

What does it mean to "honor" your parents? (To respect them.)

What does this include? (Obedience to them and treating them well.)

This is called the first commandment with a promise. What is that promise? (That those who honor their parents will live long in the land God is giving them.)

God gave this promise to His people who were on their way to the promised land. Read Ephesians 6:1–3 for the apostle Paul's version of this verse.

Does God's promise apply to believers today? (Yes.)

How? (Those who obey Him and honor their parents will do well and live long on earth.)

Week 45

Bible Memory Verse

A soft answer turneth away wrath:
but grievous words stir up anger.
Proverbs 15:1 KJV

A gentle answer turns away wrath,
but a harsh word stirs up anger.
Proverbs 15:1 NIV

A gentle answer deflects anger,
but harsh words make tempers flare.
Proverbs 15:1 NLT

About This Verse

This proverb provides a way for Christians to deal with a common problem: anger. By speaking peaceably, we can calm an angry person.

Memorization Guideline

When confronted with anger, it's hard not to respond in a like manner. But one of the ways we can love others is to keep overpowering emotions from destroying our relationships. God encourages us to deflect anger by responding with softer, thoughtful words.

Learning Tips

If you are using the King James Version and it includes an unfamiliar word, have your child look at another version for help. You may help children understand this verse by pointing out that the word *grievous* comes from our word *grief.* Harsh words cause grief to other people.

Going Deeper

What is a "gentle" or "soft" answer? (A kind and quiet response.)

What is a "harsh" or "grievous" answer? (An angry or nasty response.)

135

Have you ever responded gently to someone who was angry? What happened? (Encourage your child to share a personal experience here. If your child cannot remember responding gently, encourage this behavior and ask the child to see what happens.)

Have you responded to anger with anger? What happened? (Encourage your child to share a personal experience here.)

Why do you think God tells us to respond gently?

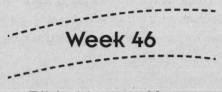

Week 46

Bible Memory Verse

Wherefore, my beloved brethren, let every man be swift to hear, slow to speak, slow to wrath: For the wrath of man worketh not the righteousness of God.
James 1:19–20 KJV

My dear brothers and sisters, take note of this: Everyone should be quick to listen, slow to speak and slow to become angry, because human anger does not produce the righteousness that God desires.
James 1:19–20 NIV

Understand this, my dear brothers and sisters: You must all be quick to listen, slow to speak, and slow to get angry. Human anger does not produce the righteousness God desires.
James 1:19–20 NLT

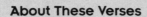

About These Verses

These verses give more of God's view of anger and how we should deal with it. It connects speech with anger, since we so often offend others with our words. By using our words wisely, we may avoid being angry and making others angry.

Memorization Guideline

If your child is prone to anger, memorizing this verse and thinking of it often could help. Frequently encourage God's anger-control method here: listen to others carefully, don't jump in with an answer, and don't let things fire off your temper. In other words, slow down.

Learning Tips

For a younger child, you may split these verses into memorization for two weeks. Use the questions that relate to each verse in the week you are memorizing each. Review the first verse before you start memorization of the second, so the second one makes more sense.

Going Deeper

What does it mean to be "quick to listen" or "swift to hear"? (To carefully listen before we respond to someone else's words.)

What does it mean to be "slow to speak"? (Not to immediately respond to another person's words, but to think about our answer first.)

What is wrath? (Strong anger or retribution.)

Does God wants us to be full of wrath? (No.)

Why not? (Because it does not bring about righteousness.)

Do you remember last week's verse? What did that teach us? (To respond gently to angry people.)

How does that verse relate to this one? (It tells us that after we have thought about what to say, we should say something gentle.)

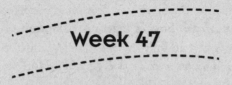

Week 47

Bible Memory Verse

But the fruit of the Spirit is love, joy, peace,
longsuffering, gentleness, goodness, faith, meekness,
temperance: against such there is no law.
Galatians 5:22–23 KJV

But the fruit of the Spirit is love, joy,
peace, forbearance, kindness, goodness,
faithfulness, gentleness and self-control.
Against such things there is no law.
Galatians 5:22–23 NIV

But the Holy Spirit produces this kind of fruit
in our lives: love, joy, peace, patience, kindness,
goodness, faithfulness, gentleness, and self-control.
There is no law against these things!
Galatians 5:22–23 NLT

About These Verses

What kind of people should we be, as Christians? Galatians 5:22–23 answers that question by describing the qualities the Spirit will develop in our lives. Becoming that kind of person is a life work, and only God's Spirit can fully develop those qualities in us.

Memorization Guideline

God can grow your child into a Christian who shows the fruit of the Spirit in daily life. After you work to memorize these words, encourage your child to cooperate with God by trying to be loving, peaceful, patient, and so on. As challenges arise, remind your child that God alone can grow the Spirit's fruit in our lives.

Learning Tips

We are like fruit trees who grow love, joy, peace, and so on as our roots go deep into God's Word and our branches rise up to Him in love. For a young child, you may prepare slips of paper with the qualities of faith written on them. Your child can draw a large tree and paste the slips of paper on it to show what fruit the Christian bears.

Going Deeper

What does God mean when He talks about "fruit"? (Good qualities that grow in our lives as the Holy Spirit works in us.)

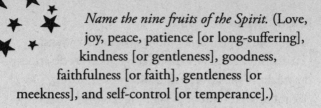

Name the nine fruits of the Spirit. (Love, joy, peace, patience [or long-suffering], kindness [or gentleness], goodness, faithfulness [or faith], gentleness [or meekness], and self-control [or temperance].)

What law is this verse talking about? (God's law—the spiritual truths He gave His people to follow. But of course there will be no other laws against these kinds of actions, either.)

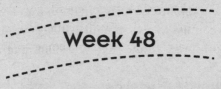

Week 48

Bible Memory Verse

Give, and it shall be given unto you; good measure,
pressed down, and shaken together, and running over,
shall men give into your bosom. For with the
same measure that ye mete withal it shall
be measured to you again.
Luke 6:38 KJV

"Give, and it will be given to you. A good measure,
pressed down, shaken together and running over,
will be poured into your lap. For with the measure
you use, it will be measured to you."
Luke 6:38 NIV

"Give, and you will receive. Your gift will return
to you in full—pressed down, shaken together
to make room for more, running over,
and poured into your lap. The amount you give
will determine the amount you get back."
Luke 6:38 NLT

About This Verse

Here God describes His generous, unlimited giving to those who love Him enough to give in return. When we give generously, we will find that we cannot outgive God.

Memorization Guideline

Today the phrase "shall men give into your bosom" is confusing. But in the first century, men wore a loose outer garment that would have bloused out at the waist. This could have formed a first-century "tote bag" that could hold grain.

Learning Tips

You may want to give your child a picture of what this verse means by taking flour and loosely pouring it into a cup measure. Then press it down with a spoon and add more on top. Press again. How much more have you added? Baking recipes often specify how the cook should treat flour to get just the right amount, because how you handle grain can substantially change the measurement. Older children may take part in this experiment to see how much more was added by weighing the grain before and after the additions.

Going Deeper

What does God tell us will happen when we give? (We will receive more than we gave.)

How can we figure the amount that we will receive? (By the amount we give.)

What does that mean? (That God will be as generous in His giving as we are in our giving.)

Does this verse make you feel like giving? Why?

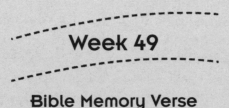

Week 49

Bible Memory Verse

Ask, and it shall be given you; seek, and ye shall find; knock, and it shall be opened unto you.
Matthew 7:7 KJV

"Ask and it will be given to you; seek and you will find; knock and the door will be opened to you."
Matthew 7:7 NIV

"Keep on asking, and you will receive what you ask for. Keep on seeking, and you will find. Keep on knocking, and the door will be opened to you."
Matthew 7:7 NLT

About This Verse
Faith takes persistence, especially in prayer. This verse (and the one that follows) encourages us to continue in prayer—asking, seeking, and knocking. There is an increased intensity in this verse, from casual asking, to seeking, then knocking at God's door to try to get our request.

Memorization Guideline
Matthew 7:9–11 compares the gifts people give their children to God's desire to give to His children. So when the good things we pray for do not happen, don't give up.

Learning Tips
Next week we will memorize Matthew 7:8, which gives a promise that goes with this verse. Older students can memorize both verses together this week, if you desire.

Going Deeper
Whom should we ask? (God.)

What should we ask for? (Anything we need that helps us achieve God's will for us. He will not give us anything that's bad for us.)

What do we seek? (Anything that helps us to do His will.).

When we knock, what might God open to us? (Spiritual truth and wisdom. When we persist in seeking Him, He may give us something we've requested for a long time.)

If we know that something is God's will, because He's told us so in the Bible, should we ever stop praying? (No.)

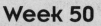

Week 50

Bible Memory Verse

For every one that asketh receiveth;
and he that seeketh findeth; and to him
that knocketh it shall be opened.
Matthew 7:8 KJV

"For everyone who asks receives; the one who
seeks finds; and to the one who knocks,
the door will be opened."
Matthew 7:8 NIV

"For everyone who asks, receives.
Everyone who seeks, finds. And to everyone
who knocks, the door will be opened."
Matthew 7:8 NLT

About This Verse

Last week God told us to ask, seek, and knock. This week He tells us the outcome of our persistent prayer.

Memorization Guideline

Your child may want to ask God for some things that are not in His will. Praying consistently for these things will not change God's mind. And the Almighty cannot be manipulated. In most cases, your child will realize that such a prayer is not right and will change that prayer. Or over time, it may become obvious that God is not going to respond.

Learning Tips

This scripture follows last week's verse. Review last week's verse and read this one aloud with it.

Going Deeper

What does God promise to those who ask? (They will receive.)

To those who seek? (They will find.)

To those who knock? (The door will be opened—they will be allowed to enter.)

What are some things that God wants us to pray for?
(Some examples are: salvation, for ourselves and others [Mark 16:15–16]; that we will grow in Him and become mature Christians [Colossians 1:10]; that we will reach out to others with our testimony of faith [Matthew 28:19]. There are many other things scripture calls us to do, and as we find them, we need to pray that they will become part of our lives.)

Can it be hard to keep on praying for the same thing?
(Yes.)

Does this verse encourage you that God is hearing your prayers, even when the answer is long in coming?

Are there some things we should not pray for with persistence? (Yes.)

What are they? (Selfish demands or things that God knows would not be good for us.)

When we realize that we've been praying this way, what can we do? (Ask God for forgiveness and start to pray differently.)

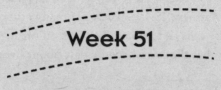

Week 51

Bible Memory Verse

Be careful for nothing; but in every thing
by prayer and supplication with thanksgiving
let your requests be made known unto God.
Philippians 4:6 KJV

Do not be anxious about anything, but in every
situation, by prayer and petition, with thanksgiving,
present your requests to God.
Philippians 4:6 NIV

Don't worry about anything; instead,
pray about everything. Tell God what you need,
and thank him for all he has done.
Philippians 4:6 NLT

About This Verse

"Don't worry" is the message God gives us with this verse. Essentially, God is saying, "Just let Me know what you need." When we have problems, we need to pray. Then we should thank Him for all He does for us.

Memorization Guideline

If your child is memorizing the King James Version, you may want to talk about the word *careful*. This does not mean that we should never care about anything or live wild lives. It means we should not be filled with cares ("care full") or worried.

Learning Tips

Next week Philippians 4:7 will be memorized. Older students may memorize the two verses together.

Going Deeper

Is there anything we need to worry about? (No.)

Why or why not? (Because God is in control of our lives, and He will take care of everything in them.)

What should we do instead of worrying? (Pray.)

When God responds to our prayers and helps us, what do we need to do? (Thank Him.)

What are some ways we can thank Him? (We can pray and tell Him how much we appreciate it, but we can also thank Him with our lives by doing things for His kingdom.)

Week 52

Bible Memory Verse

And the peace of God, which passeth
all understanding, shall keep your hearts
and minds through Christ Jesus.
Philippians 4:7 KJV

And the peace of God, which transcends
all understanding, will guard your hearts
and your minds in Christ Jesus.
Philippians 4:7 NIV

Then you will experience God's peace, which exceeds
anything we can understand. His peace will guard
your hearts and minds as you live in Christ Jesus.
Philippians 4:7 NLT

About This Verse

Last week, we learned that we should not worry but rather pray—and give thanks for God's response to our prayers. This week we learn the result that such prayer brings in our lives: peace. Even when we don't understand what's going on, we can have peace in our hearts and minds as we pray and trust in God for His answers.

Memorization Guideline

Prayer brings a deep peace to Christians and protects them, too. Though we may not understand just how it works, we can feel the peace in our lives as we trust in God no matter what. When your child becomes worried, encourage prayer as a protective problem-solver.

Learning Tips

This verse follows the verse memorized last week. Review last week's verse before you study this week's, so your child will connect the two.

Going Deeper

Last week, what did God tell us to do? (Not to worry about things, but to pray and be thankful for God's response.)

What does this week's verse promise we will have? (The peace of God.)

What is that peace like? (It passes, transcends, or exceeds all understanding.)

What does that mean? (It is beyond human understanding.)

What will God's peace do for us? (Guard our hearts and minds as we live our Christian lives.)

Additional Verses for Study

Exodus 20:1–11, 13–17
Psalm 1:3–6*
Psalm 23
Matthew 5:1–5, 7–12
Matthew 6:9–14
Matthew 10:29–31*
John 14:6
Romans 8:31–32
Ephesians 6:12–17*
Colossians 3:20
Philippians 4:4
1 Timothy 6:9–10

*Also suggested in text.

Here are exciting Bible storybooks for 8–12-year-olds—Barbour's Young Readers' Christian Library! The stories of Jesus, Jonah, Esther, and Paul are carefully retold for kids, and illustrated with line art to help you envision the characters and setting of each story. And a special "secret code" feature adds fun—as you can discover an encouraging secret message woven throughout the entire book!

Paperback / 96 pages

Wherever Christian books are sold.